Flowering of Zen in China

Origins Of ZEN

Edited & illustrated by
Tsai Chih Chung
Translated by
Koh Kok Kiang

ASIAPAC • SINGAPORE • 1990

Publisher
ASIAPAC BOOKS PTE LTD
629 Aljunied Road
#04-06 Cititech Industrial Building
Singapore 1438
Tel: 7453868
Fax: 7453822

First published Nov 1990
Reprinted Dec 1991, Nov 1992; Apr 1994, Sep 1995

© ASIAPAC BOOKS, 1990
ISBN 9971-985-55-1

Cover design by Marked Point Design
Typeset by Quaser Technology Private Limited
Printed in Singapore by Loi Printing Pte Ltd

Publisher's Note

Following the publication of the *Book of Zen*, Asiapac Comic Series now present readers with the *Origins of Zen*.

The *Book of Zen* illustrates the teachings of Zen – "Zen means to be free—absolutely—to be a human being..." – while the *Origins of Zen* traces the origins and development of Zen in China with a cheerful touch which is very much in keeping with the Zen spirit of absolute freedom and unbounded creativity.

We feel honoured to have the well-known cartoonist Tsai Chih Chung's permission to the translation right to his bestselling comics. We would also like to thank the translator and typesetter for putting in their best effort in the production of this series.

About the Editor/Illustrator

Tsai Chih Chung was born in 1948 in Chang Hwa County of Taiwan. He began drawing cartoon strips at the age of 17 and worked as Art Director for Kuang Chi Programme Service in 1971. He founded the Far East Animation Production Company and the Dragon Cartoon Production Company in 1976, where he produced two cartoon films entitled *Old Master Q* and *Shao Lin Temple*.

Tsai Chih Chung first got his four-box comics published in the newspapers and magazines in 1983. His comics such as the Drunken Swordsman, Fat Dragon, One-eyed Marshal and Bold Supersleuth were serialized in the newspapers in Singapore, Malaysia, Taiwan, Hong Kong, Japan, Europe, and the United States.

He was voted one of the Ten Outstanding Young People of Taiwan in 1985 and has been widely acclaimed by the media and the academic circle in Taiwan.

The comic book *The Sayings of Zhuang Zi* was published in 1986 and marked a milestone in Tsai's career. Within two years, *Zhuang Zi* went into more than 70 reprints in Taiwan and 15 in Hong Kong, and has to date sold over one million copies.

In 1987, Tsai Chih Chung published *The Sayings of Lao Zi, The Sayings of Confucius* and two books based on Zen. Since then, he has published more than 20 titles, out of which 10 are about ancient Chinese thinkers and the rest based on historical and literary classics. All these topped the bestsellers' list at one time or another. They have been translated into other languages such as Japanese, Korean, Thai. Asiapac is the publisher for the English version of these comics.

Tsai Chih Chung can be said to be the pioneer in the art of visualizing Chinese literature and philosophy by way of comics.

Introduction

Zen had a most unlikely reception when it first fell on Chinese ears. The 28th Indian Zen Patriarch, Bodhidharma, came to China in the year 527 and was invited to the capital of the Liang Dynasty in Nanjing. At the imperial court, he was received by Emperor Wu who, though a devout Buddhist, failed to make sense of Bodhidharma's profound utterances.

Bodhidharma left the palace and travelled to a remote hinterland of China to sit in meditation and waited until a worthy Chinese successor emerged. Thus did Zen take root in Chinese soil.

Nothing perhaps illustrates the down-to-earth Zen way of living better than the Chinese patriarchs who became its torch bearers. All of them were without exception undistinguished personalities – undistinguished, that is, by society's yardstick. One, Third Patriarch Sengcan, was a leper and another one who had the most far-reaching influence on the development of Zen in China, Sixth Patriarch Huineng, was illiterate.

Because Zen flowered in the hearts of humble people so early in its history in China, it becomes easy to understand why the Zen masters who later emerged were so scathing in dismissing intellectual humbug.

Life, after all, is meant to be lived fully in the here and now. Any pretension to knowledge about "the theory of life" negates living rather than adds to its immensity.

Tsai Chih Chung based his illustrations on various sources, principally the *Jingde Chuan Deng Lu* (Record Concerning the Passing On of the Lamp, composed in the Jingde Period), the earliest historical work of Zen literature compiled in the year 1004, and *The Golden Age of Zen* by John C.H.Wu.

Koh Kok Kiang

About the translator

Koh Kok Kiang is a journalist by vocation and a quietist by inclination. His interest in cultural topics and things of the mind started in his schooling years. It was his wish to discover the wisdom of the East that kindled his interest in Eastern philosophy. He is also the translator for the following titles in Asiapac Comic Series: *Book of Zen, Sayings of Lao Zi, Sayings of Lao Zi Book 2, Sayings of Lie Zi, Sayings of Zhuang Zi Book 2* and *The 36 Stratagems*.

Contents

Origins Of
ZEN

The light of truth

Bodhidharma comes to China

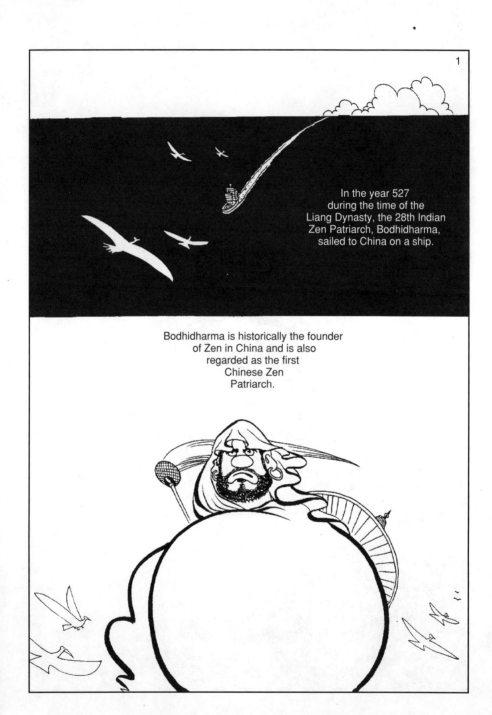

In the year 527
during the time of the
Liang Dynasty, the 28th Indian
Zen Patriarch, Bodhidharma,
sailed to China on a ship.

Bodhidharma is historically the founder
of Zen in China and is also
regarded as the first
Chinese Zen
Patriarch.

After Bodhidharma crossed the Yangtze River, he eventually went to the Shaolin Monastery on Mount Song.

15

Bodhidharma spent his days sitting in meditation and facing a wall.

16

One day, a monk named Shenguang who was earnest about learning the teaching came and stood motionless amidst the snow, waiting to meet Bodhidharma.

17

What makes you come all the way here and stand in the snow?

18

I hope Master will be compassionate and teach me the essence of Buddhism.

19

To attain buddhahood does not require a long period of practice. But if your determination is not strong, I doubt very much that you will be able to achieve it.

20

21

Urgh!

22

7

8

57 The fourth Patriarch Daoxin was succeeded by Fifth Patriarch Hongren, who in turn passed his robe of succession to Sixth Patriarch Huineng.

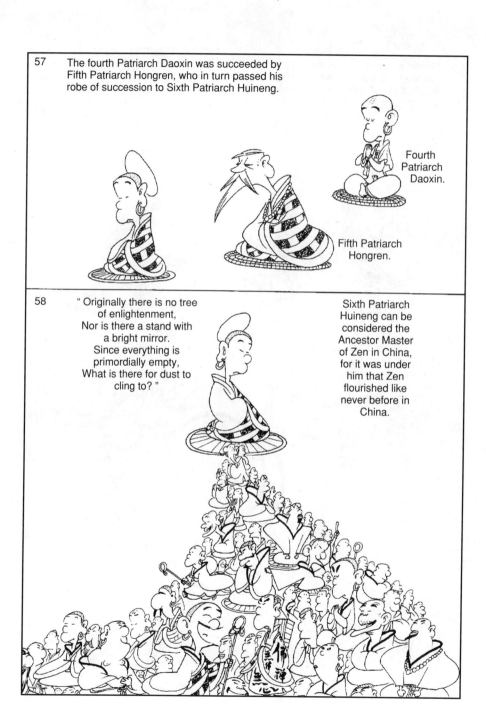

Fourth Patriarch Daoxin.

Fifth Patriarch Hongren.

58 " Originally there is no tree of enlightenment, Nor is there a stand with a bright mirror. Since everything is primordially empty, What is there for dust to cling to? "

Sixth Patriarch Huineng can be considered the Ancestor Master of Zen in China, for it was under him that Zen flourished like never before in China.

59　Geniuses are rare in any age. Yet Huineng was a genius in the same way that Lao Zi, Zhuang Zi, Confucius, and Mencius were great men.

60　His thoughts, words, and actions were recorded by his disciples in a work that was to become known as the Platform Sutra of the Sixth Patriarch. It is the only work in Chinese Buddhist literature that is accorded the status of a sutra.

61　The Platform Sutra is the product of a true man of wisdom. Every word and every phrase in it is like the refreshing water that gushes from a spring.

14

Sixth Patriarch Huineng (638-713)

Huineng's original family name was Lu. He was born in 638 and was a native of Lingnan in Guangdong province.

1

His father was an official who was dismissed from his post and banished as a commoner to Xinzhou in Lingnan. Huineng's father died when he was still a child and he lived in extreme poverty with his old mother. He sold firewood in the marketplace to earn a livelihood.

2

The Way of the Great Learning lies in illuminating the Bright Virtue.

Thus he never had an opportunity to learn how to read and write.

3

I have brought the firewood.

Just place it on that side. Here's the payment.

4

5

15

16

17

21

47 Moreover, he is just a rice-pounder who is not even literate. Let us seize the robe back from him.

Let us all give chase!

48

49 Huineng went into hiding in the forests of southern China and nobody knew his whereabouts. That is, until fifteen years later…

25

65 Yinzong shaved Huineng's head and had him ordained as a monk.

66 He himself became a disciple of Huineng.

67 Huineng began his work as a Zen master, first at the Fa Xing Monastery, then in his own, the Baolin Monastery, in Caoxi, which he established in his second year as a teacher.

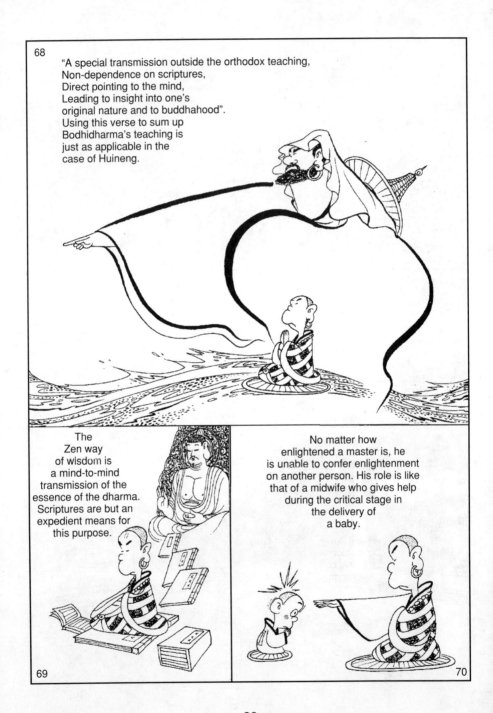

68

"A special transmission outside the orthodox teaching,
Non-dependence on scriptures,
Direct pointing to the mind,
Leading to insight into one's
original nature and to buddhahood".
Using this verse to sum up
Bodhidharma's teaching is
just as applicable in the
case of Huineng.

The Zen way of wisdom is a mind-to-mind transmission of the essence of the dharma. Scriptures are but an expedient means for this purpose.

69

No matter how enlightened a master is, he is unable to confer enlightenment on another person. His role is like that of a midwife who gives help during the critical stage in the delivery of a baby.

70

Direct pointing to the heart

Because of thought we have this idea of self and me. Because of thought, we descend to hell.

Where there is no thought, there is no good or evil, gain or loss, ignorance or wisdom, enlightenment or sorrow.

Our mind is not the source of silence, but the course of movement. Like water, it is sometimes clear and sometimes murky, sometimes still and sometimes turbulent.

The enlightened mind is like an unceasing flow and has no fixed abode.

One has to come upon the mind that does not abide anywhere.

It does not identify itself with things and therefore there is no attachment. Such a mind is the liberated mind.

31

Attaining Buddha-hood

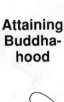

Most people regard light and darkness as two different states, but the wise man understands that in essence there is no difference.

1

Our original nature is pristine. Whether it manifests as good or bad is the result of thought.

2

If one thinks of evil, one descends to hell.

3

If one thinks of good, one enters paradise.

4

One who harbours evil thoughts becomes like a serpent (a symbol of evil) whereas one who has compassionate thoughts becomes like a bodhisattva.

5

One who is steeped in ignorance of the good will stray into evil and be unable to attain Tao. But the moment one enters the state of goodness, wisdom is born and there is the realization that buddhahood is in oneself.

6

Light and darkness, to have and not to have, good and evil, life and death are all opposite states. The original self-nature is beyond opposites, yet it includes the opposites. To enter into this dimension is to be in the state described as "original nature is buddhahood."

Non-abiding

1

It makes no difference whether one decides to leave home and become a monk or not. What is important is whether one has worldly attachments.

2

To have worldly attachments is to be like the turbulence of the waves - in an agitated state there is gain and loss and thus sorrow is born.

3

Not to have worldly attachments is to be like the calm waters. One can then have freedom of action and in this state there is no birth and death. This is the source of happiness.

4

The mind must not only abandon evil, it has to not deliberately try to cultivate goodness. It has to go beyond the duality of good and evil. Only in this way will the mind be unmoved by phenomena.

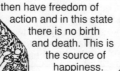

One has to keep the mind unruffled and not be affected by the fleeting phenomena around one. When the mind is unmoved, one will not be enslaved by worldly events. Be rid of duality and do not let the mind have even the slightest taint.

Gradual and instantaneous enlightenment

1

In the Tang Dynasty capital of Changan, Shenxiu enjoyed the patronage of Empress Wu Zetian and the movement he founded became known as the Northern School.

Gradual enlightenment

Instantaneous enlightenment

2

Huineng's movement became known as the Southern School. Shenxiu was an advocate of strict meditative practices such as quiet sitting and he believed this could lead to gradual enlightenment. Huineng, on the other hand, advocated instantaneous enlightenment. This was how the two schools of Zen in China had their beginnings.

3

In Huineng's school there emerged five outstanding disciples. They were Nanyue Huairang, Qingyuan Xingsi, Yongjia Xuanjue, Nanyang Huizhong, and Heze Shenhui.

Nanyue Huairang
(677 - 744)

A native of Jinzhou in Shanxi province, Huairang came from a family by the name of Du. He left home at the age of 15 and began as a novice in the Vinaya order. Later, feeling an impulse to transcend the realm of learning, he went to Mount Song to visit the Zen master Huian who, after giving him some initial instructions to broaden his mental horizons, recommended that he go south to Caoxi to visit Huineng.

Qingyuan Xingsi
(660 - 740)

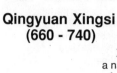

Xingsi was a native of Jizhou prefecture in Jiangxi province. His family name was Liu. Very little is known about his life except that he entered a monastery in childhood and was taciturn by nature.

Panel 1: What should a learner direct his mind to so that his attainment cannot be rated by the usual stages of progress?

Panel 2: What have you been doing of late?

Panel 3: Even the Noble Truths taught by various buddhas I shall not have anything to do with.

Panel 4: What stage of progress have you arrived at?

Panel 5: Good, good. That's very good.

What stage of progress can there be when I refuse to have anything to do even with the Noble Truths taught by the buddhas?

Panel 6: Huineng was very impressed by the depth of his insight and made him the leader of the community.

Yongjia Xuanjue
(665 - 713)

A native of Yongjia in Zhejiang province, Xuanjue came from a family named Dai. He began as a member of the Tiantai school and realized intuitively the mystery of his own mind after reading the Vimalakirti-nirdesa Sutra. On the advice of some friends, he visited Huineng to verify his insight.

1

On arrival, he circumambulated the Patriarch thrice and then, holding his staff straight, stood still before him.

2 A monk is supposed to be the embodiment of three thousand moral precepts and eighty thousand disciplinary rules. I wonder where you come from and what makes you appear to be so conceited?

The question of birth and death is of capital importance. Everything is impermanent and fleeting. I have no time to waste on ceremony.

3

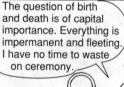

Why not embody that which is unborn and thus solve the problem of the transiency of life?

4

40

Nanyang Huizhong
(677 - 775)

Although he is listed as one of Huineng's "Big Five" disciples, there is no record to show when he visited the master and how he came to his enlightenment.

1 All that we know is that after he had his enlightenment verified by Huineng, he retired to the Baiya Mountain in Nanyang where he stayed for over forty years without once descending from the mountain.

2 In 761, he was invited by Emperor Suzong of the Tang Dynasty to the capital and honoured as a National Teacher.

3 Once during an audience, the emperor asked him many questions, but he did not even look at the emperor.

43

Heze Shenhui
(670 - 758)

Shenhui was a native of Xiangyang in Hubei province. He came from a family named Gao. As a popularizer and defender of Huineng's teaching, his merit was second to none. It was through his vigorous efforts that the Southern School of instantaneous enlightenment gained prominence over the Northern School of gradual enlightenment.

44

Mazu Daoyi (709 - 788)

Mazu came from Chengdu in Sichuan province. His family name was Ma (meaning horse). More than any other Zen master after Huineng, Mazu shaped the development of Zen in China. For this reason, he was often respectfully referred to by later Zen masters as "Ancestor Ma."

Mazu left home at the age of 12 and became a disciple of Nanyue Huairang.

In India, the 27th Patriarch Prajnatara had predicted that under your feet will come forth a spirited young horse who will trample the whole world.

After Huairang's enlightenment, Huineng told him:

1

50

The
hunter who
repented

Shigong Huicang was a hunter and he hated the sight of monks.

1

2

Once, while giving chase to his prey, he encountered Mazu.

What are you?

I am a hunter.

Do you know how to shoot?

Of course I do!

3

4

5

How many can you hit with one arrow?

One arrow can only shoot down one deer.

6

Ha! Ha! Ha! In that case, you really don't know how to shoot.

Do you know how to shoot then?

7

52

The role of two masters

1

Although Mazu and Shitou were said to "divide the world of Zen between them," they were entirely free of any sense of rivalry.

2

Yaoshan Weiyan was actually Shitou's disciple.

I hear there is a teaching about "pointing directly at the mind and attaining buddhahood through the perception of the self-nature." I humbly beseech you to enlighten me on this.

3

It is to be found neither in affirmation nor in negation nor in affirming and negating at the same time. So what would you do?

I... I do not know.

4

The cause and occasion of your enlightenment are not present in this place. You should rather go to visit the Great Master Mazu.

Yes.

Thus Yaoshan went to pay Mazu a visit.

5

Where did the wild ducks fly to?

What is that sound?

The call of wild ducks.

Mazu and his disciple Baizhang Huaihai heard the call of wild ducks while they were out for a stroll.

1

Flown away.

The call of the ducks; where have they gone?

2

Ouch! That's painful.

3

And you said, 'flown away'.

4

When the mind is like a mirror, it retains no image of whatever it reflects. When a thing is over, there is no residue of memory.

Sun-faced Buddha, Moon-faced Buddha

1

In Buddhist lore, the lifespan of the Sun-faced Buddha is one thousand eight hundred years.

2

The lifespan of the Moon-faced Buddha is only one day and one night.

3

As Mazu's death approached, the superior of the monastery came to visit him.

4

How are you doing?

5

Sun-faced Buddha, Moon-faced Buddha.

It makes not the slightest difference whether one lives long or short, so long as one understands the ground of being. That kind of life is a life of worth.

The wild fox's awakening

1. Whenever Baizhang Huaihai gave a dharma talk, a certain old man was always there listening to it together with the monks. When they left, he left too.

2. I am not a human being. Originally, I was the abbot of the temple on this mountain.

3. Who might you be?

4. No, he is not subject to causation.

Is an enlightened being still subject to the law of causation.

A certain novice monk once asked me:

5. Because I gave a wrong answer, showing a clinging to absoluteness, I have for five hundred lives been reborn as a fox.

The pure rules of Baizhang

1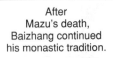
After Mazu's death, Baizhang continued his monastic tradition.

2
He was the first to lay out a set of clearly formulated rules for Zen monks, thereby securing Zen's independence from other Buddhist schools.

3
Baizhang created regulations adapted to Zen in which something of the simple, rigorous spirit of the ancient Buddhist monastic community lived on. From abbot downwards, everyone had a role to play for the common good.

Those who wished to enter a monastic community had to observe the following five rules:
Not to kill.
Not to sin sexually.
Not to steal and rob.
Not to lie or speak wildly.
Not to drink intoxicants.

4

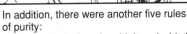

5
In addition, there were another five rules of purity:
Not to sit or sleep in a high and wide bed.
Not to wear any flower or gem on the head.
Not to sing and dance like a professional actor, or to go deliberately to watch performances.
Not to lay hold of gold and silver or any treasure.
Not to eat outside of the regular hours.

6
It is only after taking this second vow, which together with the first is called the tenfold vow of purity, that the rite of shaving the head is performed.

61

Ashes and fire

Emperor Wu Zong's suppression of Buddhism

1 In the year 845, Buddhism in China was dealt a severe blow. The emperor at that time, Wu Zong, cited economic reasons for ordering a widespread suppression of Buddhism. He issued an imperial edict to justify his actions:

2 Now, when one man does not farm, others suffer hunger and, when one woman does not weave, others suffer from the cold. At present, the monks and nuns of the empire are numberless, and they all depend on agriculture for their food and sericulture for their clothing. The monasteries and temples are beyond count, but they are all lofty and beautifully decorated, daring to rival palaces in grandeur. None other than this was the reason for the decline in material strength and the weakening of the morals of the Six Dynasties.

3 More than 4,600 monasteries and more than 40,000 temples and shrines throughout the empire were destroyed. More than 260,500 monks and nuns were returned to lay life, and 150,000 slaves were taken over by the government.

During this suppression of the Buddhist sects, only Zen managed to remain more or less unscathed.

Because Zen is not dependent on scriptures, Buddhist statues, and rituals, it could still flourish amid the destruction.

Zen monks also did their own manual work to support themselves and were not dependent on society.

Such a state of affairs can be said to be due to Baizhang's foresight in making the Zen communities self-reliant, so that during a time of calamity they could still grow steadily.

Baizhang's emphasis on the value of manual labour in a community has great relevance for humanity. In becoming self-reliant and not dependent, we hold our destiny in our own hands.

Mind is buddha.

A monk asked Guishan:

What is Tao?

The no-mind is Tao.

1.

2. I do not comprehend.

3. All you need to do is to apprehend the one who does not comprehend.

4. Who is the one who does not comprehend?

5. He is none other than yourself.

Be absolutely aware and desires will come naturally to an end. Base instincts will be transcended and there will be inner clarity. In this way one can perceive clearly one's original self.

6. If you gain bits of knowledge and information from the outside, mistaking them for Zen and Tao, you are quite off the mark. This kind of learning is like dumping dross upon your mind instead of purging it of dross. Therefore I say it is not Tao at all. Know that the one who does not comprehend is precisely your mind, precisely your buddha.

The devilry of words

* Shravaka: A hearer or disciple of Buddha who understands the Four Noble Truths, rids himself of the unreality of the phenomenal world, and enters a nirvana that is not fully mature.

Not living in vain

Once, Yangshan paid a visit to Guishan after being absent for a time.

My son, I have not seen you for the whole summer. What work have you accomplished?

Well, I have tilled a strip of land and planted a basketful of seeds.

Then you have not passed the summer in idleness.

And what have you been doing, master?

Taking a meal at midday and sleeping in the night.

So you too, master, have not passed the summer in idleness.

There is no essential difference between vigorous, complex action and quiet, simple action. So long as one uses the non-discriminating ordinary mindfulness in every-day living, then one would not have lived in idleness. Both vigour and quietude have their good qualities.

Self and other

Once, when Yangshan was staying at Dongping, Guishan sent someone to present him with a letter and a mirror.

1

Can you tell me whether this mirror belongs to Guishan or me? If you say it is mine, the fact is that Guishan gave it to me.

2

If you say it is Guishan's, the fact is that it has been given to me. If anyone can give an answer, I will not smash the mirror.

3

4

Yangshan repeated his question thrice but received no answer. So he smashed the mirror.

The enlightened being is one with everything, with no distinction of self and other. Life then has no past and present and pervades all.

Zhaozhou Congshen
(778 - 897)

Zhaozhou came from a family named He of Caozhou district in Shandong province. He began as a novice in a local monastery before travelling to visit Master Nanquan in Anhui province.

1 It happened that at the time of his arrival, Nanquan was resting, stretched out on his back on his couch.

2 Where do you come from?

From Ruixiang (Holy Image) Monastery.

3 Do you still see the Holy Image?

No, I do not see it.

4 But just now I saw the sleeping Tathagatha!

5 Are you a free monk or one belonging to a master?

73

74

Kicked by an ass

After his enlightenment, Zhaozhou spent many years travelling and visiting contemporary Zen masters to exchange insights with them.

1

Once, he visited the monk Zhuyou.

A man of your age should try to find a place to settle down and teach.

2

Where is my abiding place?

3

What? You don't even realize that the True Man is his own abiding place?

4

For thirty years I have roamed freely on horseback. Today, for the first time I am kicked by an ass!

5

What the monk said was so obvious a truth as to make its articulation quite silly. Hence in pointing out the errors of others one may not realize that oneself may be the source of errors.

76

Zhaozhou was about eighty when he settled down at the Guan Yin Monastery in Zhaozhou district.

6

7

When he became abbot at the monastery, his profound wisdom attracted many disciples from afar and he had thirteen dharma successors.

8

If a seven-year-old child is smarter than me, I will learn from him. If a hundred-year-old person is not my equal, I will teach him.

When the heart is pure, all is pure

Tao has no fixed abode. The usefulness of the brain cannot be said to be greater than that of one's intestines. Both are of equal importance.

One day, a nun asked Zhaozhou:

Can you tell me the secret of all secrets (that is, the fundamental truth)?

There it is!

Gosh!

I am shocked that you still have got that in you.

Rather it is you who have still got that in you. When the heart is pure, all is pure. When the heart is impure, all is impure.

!

Zhaozhou was free from sexual desire, but the nun thought he still had it. What Zhaozhou was trying to point out was that the fundamental truth can be found within herself.

The big turnips of Zhenzhou

Teacher, I have heard that you have personally seen Master Nanquan and became his dharma successor. Is this true?

Zhenzhou produces big turnips.*

Hearsay is just hearsay, unless one has personally seen a thing, it is not to be believed. Belief or non-belief has nothing to do with hearsay; the key to understanding is in oneself. One who pays attention only to knowledge from outside will lose sight of one's own potential.

*At that time, it was a well-known fact that Zhenzhou had always produced big turnips.
Similarly, everyone in Zen circles knew that Zhaozhou had called on Nanquan. The question was superfluous.

83

Tianhuang Daowu
(748 - 807)

A native of Wuzhou in Zhejiang province, Tianhuang Daowu came from a family by the name of Zhang. He left for Hangzhou when he was fifteen to become a monk and later became a student of Jingshan Daoqin, an outstanding Zen master in the lineage of Fourth Patriarch Daoxin.

After serving Jingshan for five years, he went to visit Mazu, who confirmed his insights.

1

2

After spending two years with Mazu, he went to visit Shitou Xiqian.

After one is freed of dhyana and prajna, what dharma can one show to others?

In my place there are no slaves, so what is there to be freed from?

3

How is this to be verified?

4

Can you grasp at emptiness?

5

This ungraspability does not begin today.

6

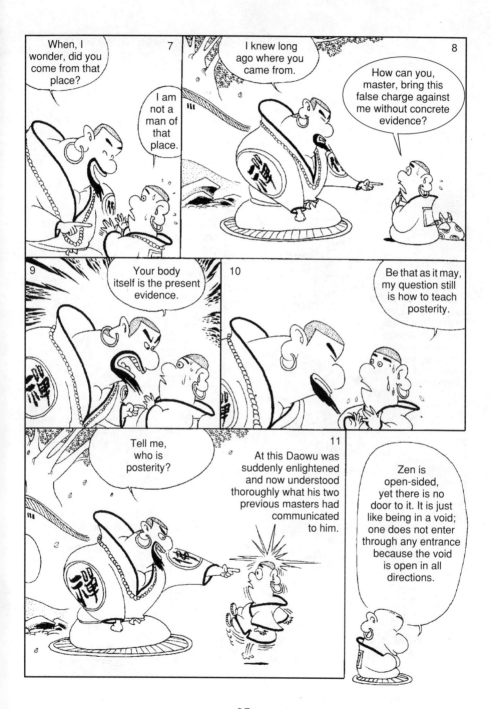

Bodhisattva Shanhui (497-)

Shanhui, better known as Fu Da Shi, was one of the most extraordinary figures in Buddhism and an important precursor of the School of Zen.

1 Once he was invited by Emperor Wu of Liang (who reigned from 502 to 549) to give a lecture on the Diamond Sutra.

Rap!

2 No sooner had he ascended to the platform than he rapped the table and descended.

I don't understand at all.

Does Your Majesty understand?

3

4 But I have already finished my sermon.

Buddhahood, Tao, and Zen are beyond words, and because language is employed to describe them, there is deviation from the actual. Hence, not to preach the dharma is to show it.

Host and guest unchanged

One day, while Shanhui was delivering a sermon, Emperor Wu arrived and the whole community rose to show their respect. Only Shanhui remained seated.

Here comes His Majesty!

Why don't you stand up when His Majesty has come?

If the realm of the dharma is unsettled, the whole world would lose its peace.

One who makes distinctions of respect and disdain, high and low status, the big and the small will be unable to perceive the truth underlying all things.

Unity
of three
philosophies

One day,
wearing a Buddhist
cassock, a Taoist cap, and
Confucian shoes, Shanhui
entered the imperial court.

Taoist cap

Buddhist cassock

Confucian shoes

1

2

Are you a Buddhist monk?

Are you then a Taoist priest?

Shanhui pointed to his cap.

3

4

Shanhui pointed to his shoes.

So you are a man of the world?

5

With a Taoist cap, a Buddhist cassock, and a pair of Confucian shoes, I have harmonized three houses into one big family.

Ah…

Being non-sectarian, Zen can be considered a harmony of Buddhism, Taoism and Confucianism. It is applicable to daily living.

6

Shanhui pointed to his cassock.

7

91

Dongshan Liangjie
(807 - 869)

Dongshan was a native of Guiji in Zhejiang province. His family name was Yu. He became a monk early in life. After his enlightenment, he founded the Cao-Dong House of Zen.

1. No desire, no sorrow, no thought, no motion, no knowledge...

While Dongshan was a novice monk, his master taught him to recite the Prajna-hrdaya Sutra:

2. There is no eye, ear, nose, tongue, body or mind... no colour, sound or taste...

3. I do have eyes, ears, nose, tongue, and so forth. How, then, can the sutra say that there are no such things?

4. I suggest you find out from somebody else. I am not worthy to be your teacher.

93

94

95

Fayan Wenyi
(885 - 958)

Fayan Wenyi was a native of Yuhang in Zhejiang province and his family name was Lu. A lover of learning, he steeped himself in the Buddhist scriptures. He was the founder of the Fayan House of Zen.

Urged by a mystic impetus stirring in him, Fayan embarked on a journey to seek the instruction of Zen masters. As he was passing by the monastery of Di Cang, he was caught in a snowstorm, so that he had to stop over for a while.

1

The abbot, Lohan Guicheng asked him:

What is the destination of your present trip?

I am only a pilgrim.

2

3

What is the meaning of your pilgrimage?

I don't know.

4

Unknowing is closest to it.

5

It has stopped snowing and I ought to leave.

A drop of water from Caoxi

1

After Sixth Patriarch Huineng was ordained, he went to Caoxi where he established the Baolin Monastery. He stayed there for 36 years and Caoxi was later revered as a holy ground of Zen.

2

What is the meaning of a drop of water from the source at Caoxi?

3

A drop of water from the source at Caoxi.

!

How are you? How are you?

When using words to answer a question, there is bound to be some inadequacy. The most complete answer is usually in the question itself. Reality and its symbol can be said to be one. The word is the pointer and the thing pointed to is the word's denotation.

Formless Void

Panel 1: Fayan asked his disciple Yongming Daoqian:
"Which sutra are you reading?"
"The Buddhavatamsaka Sutra."

Panel 2: "The six attributes of being* – in what part of the sutra is this subject treated?"
"It is treated under the section on The Ten Stages. But logically speaking, the six attributes are universally applicable."

Panel 3: "Does Sunyata or Formless Void possess the six attributes?"
"I don't know..."

Panel 4: "Suppose you ask me the same question."

Panel 5: "Does the Formless Void possess the six attributes?"

Panel 6: "Formless Void!"

Panel 7: "How do you understand it?"
"Thank you, master, I finally have understood."

Panel 8: "Formless Void!"
"Wonderful!"
"The unseen force that created the universe is a most invaluable thing. Its progress lies in simple everyday happenings. Any method or technique that is too complex will only give rise to complications."

---

* The universal and the particular, the same and the different, the positive and the negative.

Yunmen Wenyan
(864 - 949)

Yunmen Wenyan was a native of Jiaxin in Zhejiang province. He came from a poor family by the name of Zhang. When he was a mere boy, his parents placed him in the hands of a Vinaya master to be a novice monk. He was the founder of the Yunmen House of Zen.

One day, he paid a visit to Zen master Muzhou Daoming.

1

2

Who are you?

My name is Wenyan.

3

What do you want?

I am not yet enlightened on the problem of my own Self, and I have come to beg for your instruction.

Muzhou opened the door but, after a quick look at him, shut it again.

4

5

In the following two days, Yunmen knocked on the door and met with the same experience.

On the third day...

100

One-word pass

Yunmen is famous in Zen history for his use of the "one-word pass." This is a tactic he used to awaken the dormant potentiality of his disciples.

Pass!

? !

1

What is the treasury of the eye of the true dharma?

Universal!

How do you look at the wonderful coincidence between the chick tapping inside its shell and the hen's pecking from outside?

Echo!

Personal experience.

What is the one road of Yunmen?

2

3

4

When you kill your father and mother, you repent before the Buddha; when you kill the Buddha and the Patriarchs, where do you turn to repent?

Exposed!

What is Tao?

Go!

Where our late teacher remained silent when a question was put to him, how shall we enter it in the epitaph?

Teacher!

5

6

7

There is no particular magic in the one-word pass of Yunmen. One word or many words, there is always the pass for one to break through.

It is just one of the ways of evoking the incommunicable.

8

Language has limitations whereas truth has none. To try to apprehend the truth through language is to stray further and further away from it.

Yunmen's three attributes

Yunmen's three attributes on the truth underlying everything are:

Omnipresence: Permeating and covering the whole cosmic order.

Transcendence: Cutting off once and for all the flow of all streams.

Indwelling: Following the waves and keeping up with the currents.

All these three ultimately refer to the Absolute. They represent its three aspects as we view it.

Looking at its omnipresence, we find that it pervades and covers the whole cosmos and all its parts.

In its transcendence, it is infinitely higher than the cosmos, alone and peerless, in no way approachable by any being in the world.

But in the end we see the great return. For it exists or resides in all things as their moving force (indwelling).

The Absolute can be found in the fire.

104

House of Linji

House of Gui-Yang

The House of Cao-Dong

Huineng's Southern School of Zen branched out into five "houses" towards the end of the Tang Dynasty. From Nanyue Huairang's lineage came the House of Gui-Yang and the House of Linji. From the lineage of Qingyuan Xingsi emerged the House of Cao-Dong, Yunmen and Fayan. They collectively became the Five Houses of Zen.

The House of Fayan

The House of Yunmen

Of the Five Houses of Zen, that of Gui-Yang, Yunmen and Fayan died out after the Song Dynasty. Only the Linji and Cao-Dong Houses continued to flourish. Of the two, the Cao-Dong House was more prominent.

106

Glossary

Buddha
It means "awakened one". Any person who is enlightened is a buddha. The founder of Buddhism, Shakyamuni Buddha or Guatama Buddha as he is known, is not the first and only buddha.

Buddha-nature
According to Zen, it is the true, immutable and eternal nature of all beings. Since all beings possess this buddha-nature, it is possible for everyone to realize it.

Buddhahood
The expression for the realization of perfect enlightenment, which characterizes a buddha.

Bodhisattva
A being who is awakened but postpones entry into complete nirvana out of compassion for others who are living in delusion.

Dharma
It is the universal truth underlying all things. It also refers to the teaching of the historical Buddha, Shakyamuni; thus the teaching that expresses the universal truth.

Dhyana
In Chinese Buddhism, it refers to all meditative practices as the way to enlightenment.

Gatha
In Zen, a verse composed to express the moment of insight.

Nirvana
In Zen, nirvana is the realization of the true essence of the mind. The mind in which the ego ceases to exist is the universal mind.

Prajna
It means wisdom. The definitive moment of prajna is insight into the emptiness of thought or consciousness.

Sutra
Discourses of the historical Buddha. According to tradition, they derive directly from the Buddha and have been preserved in Sanskrit and Pali as well as Chinese and Tibetan translations.

Sangha
Monastic community.

Asiapac Comic Series (by Tsai Chih Chung)

Art of War
Translated by Leong Weng Kam
The Art of War provides a compact set of principles essential for victory in battles; applicable to military strategists, in business and human relationships.

Book of Zen
Translated by Koh Kok Kiang
Zen makes the art of spontaneous living the prime concern of the human being. Tsai depicts Zen with unfettered versatility; his illustrations spans a period of more than 2,000 years.

Da Xue
Translated by Mary Ng En Tzu
The second book in the Four Books of the Confucian Classics. It sets forth the higher principles of moral science and advocates that the cultivation of the person be the first thing attended to in the process of the pacification of kingdoms.

Fantasies of the Six Dynasties
Translated by Jenny Lim
Tsai Chih Chung has creatively illustrated and annotated 19 bizarre tales of human encounters with supernatural beings which were compiled during the Six Dyansties (AD 220-589).

Lun Yu
Translated by Mary Ng En Tzu
A collection of the discourses of Confucius, his disciples and others on various topics. Several bits of choice sayings have been illustrated for readers in this book.

New Account of World Tales
Translated by Alan Chong
These 120 selected anecdotes tell the stories of emperors, princes, high officials, generals, courtiers, urbane monks and lettered gentry of a turbulent time. They afford a stark and amoral insight of human behaviour in its full spectrum of virtues and frailties and glimpses of brilliant Chinese witticisms, too.

Origins of Zen
Translated by Koh Kok Kiang
  Tsai in this book traces the origins and development of Zen in China with a light-hearted touch which is very much in keeping with the Zen spirit of absolute freedom and unbounded creativity.

Records of the Historian
Translated by Tang Nguok Kiong
  Adapted from Records of the Historian, one of the greatest historical work China has produced, Tsai has illustrated the life and characteristics of the Four Lords of the Warring Strates.

Roots of Wisdom
Translated by Koh Kok Kiang
  One of the gems of Chinese literature, whose advocacy of a steadfast nature and a life of simplicity, goodness, quiet joy and harmony with one's fellow beings and the world at large has great relevance in an age of rapid changes.

Sayings of Confucius
Translated by Goh Beng Choo
  This book features the life of Confucius, selected sayings from The Analects and some of his more prominent pupils. It captures the warm relationship between the sage and his disciples, and offers food for thought for the modern readers.

Sayings of Han Fei Zi
Translated by Alan Chong
  Tsai Chih Chung retold and interpreted the basic ideas of legalism, a classical political philosophy that advocates a draconian legal code, embodying a system of liberal reward and heavy penalty as the basis of government, in his unique style.

Sayings of Lao Zi
Translated by Koh Kok Kiang & Wong Lit Khiong
  The thoughts of Lao Zi, the founder of Taoism, are presented here in a light-hearted manner. It features the selected sayings from Dao De Jing.

Sayings of Lao Zi Book 2
Translated by Koh Kok Kiang

In the second book, Tsai Chih Chung has tackled some of the more abstruse passages from the Dao De Jing which he has not included in the first volume of Sayings of Lao Zi.

Sayings of Lie Zi
Translated by Koh Kok Kiang

A famous Taoist sage whose sayings deals with universal themes such as the joy of living, reconciliation with death, the limitations of human knowledge, the role of chance events.

Sayings of Mencius
Translated by Mary Ng En Tzu

This book contains stories about the life of Mencius and various excerpts from "Mencius", one of the Four Books of the Confucian Classics, which contains the philosophies of Mencius.

Sayings of Zhuang Zi
Translated by Goh Beng Choo

Zhuang Zi's non-conformist and often humorous views of life have been creatively illustrated and simply presented by Tsai Chih Chung in this book.

Sayings of Zhuang Zi Book 2
Translated by Koh Kok Kiang

Zhuang Zi's book is valued for both its philosophical insights and as a work of great literary merit. Tsai's second book on Zhuang Zi shows maturity in his unique style.

Strange Tales of Liaozhai
Translated by Tang Nguok Kiong

In this book, Tsai Chih Chung has creatively illustrated 12 stories from the Strange Tales of Liaozhai, an outstanding Chinese classic written by Pu Songling in the early Qing Dynasty.

Zhong Yong
Translated by Mary Ng En Tzu

Zhong Yong, written by Zi Si, the grandson of Confucius, gives voice to the heart of the discipline of Confucius. Tsai has presented it in a most readable manner for the modern readers to explore with great delight.

Strategy & Leadership Series by Wang Xuanming

Thirty-six Stratagems: Secret Art of War
Translated by Koh Kok Kiang (cartoons) &
Liu Yi (text of the stratagems)
A Chinese military classic which emphasizes deceptive schemes to achieve military objectives. It has attracted the attention of military authorities and general readers alike.

Six Strategies for War: The Practice of Effective Leadership
Translated by Alan Chong
A powerful book for rulers, administrators and leaders, it covers critical areas in management and warfare including: how to recruit talents and manage the state; how to beat the enemy and build an empire; how to lead wisely; and how to manoeuvre brilliantly.

Gems of Chinese Wisdom: Mastering the Art of Leadership
Translated by Leong Weng Kam
Wise up with this delightful collection of tales and anecdotes on the wisdom of great men and women in Chinese history, including Confucius, Meng Changjun and Gou Jian.

Three Strategies of Huang Shi Gong: The Art of Government
Translated by Alan Chong
Reputedly one of man's oldest monograph on military strategy, it unmasks the secrets behind brilliant military manoeuvres, clever deployment and control of subordinates, and effective government.

100 Strategies of War: Brilliant Tactics in Action
Translated by Yeo Ai Hoon
The book captures the essence of extensive military knowledge and practice, and explores the use of psychology in warfare, the importance of building diplomatic relations with the enemy's neighbours, the use of espionage and reconnaissance, etc.

《亚太漫画系列》

六祖坛经

编著：蔡志忠

翻译：许国强

亚太图书（新）有限公司出版

25/3/88